The Focus Funnel

The Focus Funnel

Petchinsky

The Focus Funnel: How to Cut Through Chaos and Get Results
By: Matthew Petchinsky

Introduction

In a world brimming with distractions, achieving focus has become both a rare skill and an invaluable asset. From the constant barrage of notifications to the overwhelming number of tasks competing for our attention, the modern individual faces unprecedented challenges to stay focused. Yet, amidst this chaos, focus remains the key to achieving more in less time. It is not merely a productivity hack; it is the foundation for clarity, purpose, and accomplishment in every aspect of life.

The truth is, time is finite. We all have the same 24 hours in a day, yet some people seem to accomplish remarkable feats while others struggle to make it through their to-do lists. The difference lies not in the quantity of time but in how that time is managed. At the heart of this success is focus—the ability to channel energy and attention toward the tasks that truly matter while filtering out distractions.

Why Focus is the Key to Achieving More in Less Time

Focus is not just about working harder or longer hours; it is about working smarter. When you focus, you align your actions with your goals, eliminating unnecessary efforts that drain energy and time. By concentrating on one task at a time, you achieve greater efficiency, higher-quality results, and a sense of fulfillment that comes from meaningful progress.

Consider how multitasking, often glorified as a way to increase productivity, actually fractures attention and diminishes performance. Research shows that switching between tasks increases cognitive load and reduces efficiency. Focus, on the other hand, creates a state of flow—a mental state where you are fully immersed in an activity, performing at your peak potential.

Moreover, focus fosters clarity. When you take the time to prioritize what truly matters, you cut through the noise and direct your efforts toward actions that bring the most value. This approach not only saves time but also reduces stress and prevents burnout, as you are no longer trying to do everything at once.

The ability to focus is like a muscle; it can be trained and strengthened. And just as with physical exercise, having the right tools and strategies is essential. This is where the Focus Funnel method comes into play—a revolutionary framework designed to help you systematically filter and prioritize tasks, ensuring that your time and energy are spent on what truly matters.

The Focus Funnel Method

The Focus Funnel method is a powerful tool that transforms how you approach your workload. It is a step-by-step process that helps you evaluate tasks, eliminate unnecessary distractions, and concentrate your efforts where they will have the greatest impact. At its core, the Focus Funnel encourages you to ask three critical questions about every task you face:

1. **Can it be eliminated?**

   Many of the tasks that clutter our lives are not essential. The first step in the Focus Funnel is to identify and eliminate activities that do not contribute to your goals. By removing these distractions, you free up valuable time and energy for more meaningful pursuits.

2. **Can it be automated?**

   If a task cannot be eliminated, the next step is to consider whether it can be automated. With advancements in technology, many repetitive tasks can be streamlined using tools and systems, allowing you to focus on higher-priority work.

3. **Can it be delegated?**

   For tasks that cannot be eliminated or automated, delegation is key. By entrusting others with responsibilities that do not require your personal involvement, you create space to focus on what only you can do.

Tasks that survive these three filters—those that cannot be eliminated, automated, or delegated—are the ones that deserve your direct attention. The Focus Funnel helps you streamline your workload, ensuring that you spend your time on the tasks that align with your goals and deliver the highest returns.

This method is not just about getting things done; it is about achieving meaningful results. By applying the Focus Funnel, you move from being reactive—constantly putting out fires and responding to immediate demands—to being proactive, purposefully directing your efforts toward long-term success.

The Promise of Focus

This book is your guide to unlocking the transformative power of focus. Through practical strategies, actionable insights, and real-world examples, you will learn how to harness the Focus Funnel method to reclaim your time, amplify your productivity, and achieve your goals with greater ease and efficiency. By mastering focus, you will not only accomplish more in less time but also experience a profound sense of purpose and satisfaction in all areas of your life.

Let this be the beginning of your journey toward a more focused, productive, and fulfilling life. Together, we will explore how to filter the noise, prioritize what matters, and create a life where focus leads the way to extraordinary achievements.

Chapter 1: Understanding the Chaos

In our fast-paced and hyper-connected world, distractions have become a constant companion. They lurk in our pockets, pop up on our screens, and infiltrate our thoughts, silently derailing our progress without us even realizing it. To master focus, the first step is understanding the chaos—how distractions undermine our productivity and how to identify the personal traps that keep us from achieving our goals. This chapter delves deep into the nature of distractions, why they hold such power over us, and how to recognize and combat them effectively.

Why Distractions Derail Progress

Distractions are more than minor annoyances; they are productivity thieves. They fragment your attention, pull you away from meaningful work, and reduce your ability to stay on track. But why do they have such a profound impact on progress?

Cognitive Overload

The human brain has a limited capacity for processing information at any given moment. When distractions interrupt your workflow, they overload your cognitive resources, making it harder to focus on the task at hand. This leads to decreased efficiency, increased errors, and mental fatigue.

For instance, receiving a single notification on your phone while working on an important project might seem harmless. However, studies have shown that even brief interruptions can have lingering effects, forcing your brain to "reset" and refocus each time you return to the task.

1. **The Illusion of Multitasking**

   Multitasking is often touted as a productivity skill, but in reality, it is a focus killer. When you attempt to juggle multiple tasks at once, your brain rapidly switches between them rather than processing them simultaneously. This switching drains mental energy, slows you down, and reduces the quality of your work. Over time, multitasking can also increase stress and decrease your ability to concentrate.

2. **The Dopamine Trap**

   Distractions, especially those delivered through technology, are designed to exploit the brain's reward system. Every time you check your phone, scroll through social media, or respond to an email, your brain releases a small hit of dopamine, the "feel-good" chemical. This creates a feedback loop that makes distractions addictive, pulling you away from more meaningful tasks in favor of short-term gratification.

3. **The Cost of Context Switching**

   Each time you switch from one task to another, your brain requires time to adjust and reorient itself. This process, known as context switching, can cost up to 40% of your productive time. The more frequently you allow distractions to interrupt your work, the less effective you become at completing tasks efficiently.

4. **Erosion of Momentum**

   Focus builds momentum. When you are deeply immersed in a task, you enter a state of flow, where your productivity and creativity peak. Distractions break this flow, forcing you to start over and rebuild the momentum you had previously gained. Over time, these interruptions can lead to frustration, procrastination, and a lack of motivation.

Recognizing Your Personal Focus Traps

Not all distractions come from external sources like phones or coworkers. Many of them originate within ourselves, driven by habits, thought patterns, and environmental triggers. Identifying your personal focus traps is essential for overcoming them and reclaiming your ability to concentrate.

1. **The Myth of "Busy Equals Productive"**

   Many people equate being busy with being productive, filling their days with low-priority tasks that do not contribute to their long-term goals. This focus trap keeps you in a cycle of doing instead of achieving. To break free, it's essential to differentiate between tasks that are urgent and those that are truly important.

2. **Procrastination and Avoidance**

   Procrastination is often a response to tasks that feel overwhelming, boring, or unclear. Instead of tackling these tasks head-on, we seek distractions as a way to avoid discomfort. Recognizing when you are using distractions to procrastinate is the first step toward overcoming this trap.

3. **Perfectionism as a Distraction**

   Striving for perfection can become a form of self-sabotage, where you spend excessive time refining minor details instead of focusing on completing the task. This focus trap delays progress and keeps you from moving forward.

4. **Overcommitting and the Fear of Saying No**

   Taking on too many responsibilities can spread your focus too thin, leaving you unable to give your best effort to any single task. Learning to say no to distractions, commitments, and obligations that do not align with your priorities is critical for maintaining focus.

5. **Unstructured Time and Lack of Prioritization**

   Without a clear plan for how to spend your time, it is easy to fall into the trap of reactive work—responding to emails, attending unnecessary meetings, or handling interruptions. Recognizing the need for structure and prioritization is key to avoiding this trap.

6. **Emotional Distractions**

   Stress, anxiety, and emotional turmoil can pull your attention away from tasks and diminish your ability to focus. Recognizing these internal distractions and addressing their root causes through mindfulness, self-care, or professional support can help you regain control.

7. **Environmental Triggers**

   Your surroundings play a significant role in your ability to focus. Cluttered workspaces, noisy environments, and easy access to distractions like social media can all hinder your concentration. Identifying and minimizing these environmental triggers can create a more focus-friendly space.

The Path Forward

Understanding why distractions derail progress and identifying your personal focus traps is the first step in reclaiming your attention. In the chapters ahead, we will explore practical strategies for minimizing distractions, mastering the art of focus, and implementing the Focus Funnel method to prioritize what truly matters. By addressing the chaos head-on, you will lay the foundation for a more productive, purposeful, and fulfilling life.

Let this chapter serve as a wake-up call—a reminder that while distractions may be inevitable, they do not have to control your life. By recognizing their impact and taking proactive steps to counter them, you can break free from the chaos and unlock your full potential.

Chapter 2: Simplify to Amplify

One of the greatest secrets to achieving more in life is learning to do less—but with intention. Simplification isn't about reducing effort; it's about magnifying your impact by focusing on what truly matters. In this chapter, we'll explore how to declutter your priorities, identify high-impact tasks, and adopt a streamlined approach that allows you to amplify your results with less stress and more clarity.

Decluttering Your Priorities

In today's world, it's easy to feel overwhelmed by the sheer number of responsibilities and expectations that demand your time and energy. The first step toward achieving focus is decluttering your priorities—distinguishing between what is essential and what is extraneous.

1. **The Power of Saying No**

   Every "yes" you give to one thing is a "no" to something else. Often, we say yes to tasks, commitments, or opportunities out of a sense of obligation, fear of disappointing others, or the allure of being busy. To simplify your priorities, you must embrace the power of saying no to anything that does not align with your goals or values.

Action Tip:

Create a "Not-To-Do List" of tasks, commitments, or habits that consume your time without providing meaningful returns. This list serves as a reminder of what to avoid, freeing you to focus on what truly matters.

2.The 80/20 Rule (Pareto Principle)

The Pareto Principle states that 80% of your results come from 20% of your efforts. Decluttering your priorities begins with identifying the 20% of tasks, projects, or activities that yield the greatest outcomes. Conversely, it's essential to recognize the 80% of activities that contribute minimally to your success and gradually phase them out.

Action Tip:

Reflect on your recent accomplishments. What specific actions or projects had the most significant impact? Focus on replicating those and eliminating tasks that did not drive meaningful results.

3.Understanding Your Core Values

Your priorities should align with your core values—those principles and beliefs that matter most to you. When you align your tasks and goals with your values, you create a sense of purpose and direction, making it easier to let go of distractions and low-priority activities.

Action Tip:

Write down your top five core values and assess whether your current priorities align with them. Adjust your to-do list to ensure that you are dedicating time and energy to what resonates with your values.

4.Batching and Bundling Tasks

Clutter often arises from scattered efforts—trying to address every task as it comes up. Batching similar tasks together allows you to focus your energy and minimize the cognitive load of switching contexts.

Example:

Instead of responding to emails throughout the day, set aside two dedicated time blocks for email management. This approach reduces interruptions and ensures that your energy is concentrated on more impactful work.

How to Identify High-Impact Tasks

High-impact tasks are the activities that move the needle—those that bring you closer to your goals with the least amount of effort and time. But how do you identify these tasks amidst the noise?

1. **Start with the End in Mind**

   To identify high-impact tasks, you need to define what success looks like. What are your long-term goals? What milestones do you need to achieve to get there? By working backward from your ultimate objectives, you can pinpoint the actions that will have the most significant impact.

Action Tip:

Use the **SMART Goals** framework to set clear, measurable goals. Once you have defined your goals, break them down into actionable steps and identify the ones with the highest leverage.

2.The Eisenhower Matrix

The Eisenhower Matrix is a powerful tool for categorizing tasks based on urgency and importance.

- **Urgent and Important:** Tasks that require immediate attention and contribute to your goals. These are your high-impact tasks.
- **Not Urgent but Important:** Tasks that are essential for long-term success but can be scheduled.
- **Urgent but Not Important:** Tasks that demand attention but do not align with your priorities. Delegate or minimize these.
- **Not Urgent and Not Important:** Eliminate these tasks altogether.

Action Tip:
At the start of each week, use the Eisenhower Matrix to categorize your tasks and prioritize accordingly.

3.Assess ROI (Return on Investment)
Not all tasks are created equal. Some provide a much higher return on your time, energy, or resources. To identify high-impact tasks, evaluate the ROI of each activity.

Questions to Ask:

-
  - Does this task contribute to my long-term goals?
  - Will this task yield significant results compared to the time and effort required?
  - Is this task aligned with my values and priorities?

Example:
Writing a report that influences a major decision in your company may have a higher ROI than spending hours designing a presentation for a minor meeting.

1. **Leverage the Focus Funnel Method**
   The Focus Funnel method, introduced in the previous chapter, can be applied here to filter and prioritize your tasks. Use it to systematically eliminate, automate, or delegate low-impact tasks, leaving only those that deserve your full attention.

2. **Listen to Your Energy Levels**
   High-impact tasks often require deep focus and creativity, which are tied to your energy levels. Identify your peak productivity hours—times when you feel most alert and motivated—and schedule your most critical tasks during those windows.

Action Tip:
Track your energy levels throughout the day for a week to discover your

natural rhythms. Use this data to create a schedule that maximizes your focus and effectiveness.

Simplification in Practice

Simplifying your priorities and focusing on high-impact tasks is not a one-time event; it is an ongoing practice. Life constantly presents new opportunities, challenges, and distractions. By adopting a mindset of simplification, you can continually refine your focus and amplify your results.

- **Review Regularly:** Set aside time each week to evaluate your priorities and adjust your plan as needed.
- **Celebrate Progress:** Acknowledge the completion of high-impact tasks to reinforce the value of focus and effort.
- **Stay Flexible:** While simplification provides structure, allow room for flexibility and adaptability when unexpected opportunities or challenges arise.

The Ripple Effect of Simplification

When you simplify your priorities, the benefits extend beyond productivity. You gain clarity, reduce stress, and create more space for creativity and innovation. By focusing on high-impact tasks, you not only achieve your goals faster but also experience a deeper sense of purpose and fulfillment.

Simplify to amplify—it's not just a strategy; it's a mindset that empowers you to cut through the noise, focus on what matters most, and create a life of extraordinary impact. As we move forward, the tools and strategies in this book will build upon this foundation, helping you transform simplification into a way of life.

Chapter 3: The Power of Deep Work

In a world where multitasking and constant connectivity are the norms, the ability to engage in deep work has become a rare and invaluable skill. Deep work refers to the state of uninterrupted, focused effort on cognitively demanding tasks. This chapter explores the transformative power of deep work, providing techniques to achieve flow states and strategies to schedule focused work time, enabling you to unlock your full potential and produce extraordinary results.

The Science Behind Deep Work

Deep work isn't just a productivity strategy; it's a neurological phenomenon. When you engage in deep work, your brain enters a state of heightened focus where distractions fade away, creativity flourishes, and your output reaches its peak. This state, often called **flow**, is characterized by:

1. **Complete Immersion:**
   You become fully absorbed in the task, losing track of time and external distractions.

2. **Increased Efficiency:**
   Cognitive resources are directed solely toward the task, maximizing performance and reducing errors.

3. **Enhanced Creativity:**
   Flow states unlock the brain's ability to connect ideas, solve problems, and think innovatively.

4. **Sense of Fulfillment:**
   Deep work fosters a sense of accomplishment and purpose, as you engage with meaningful and challenging tasks.

Despite its benefits, achieving deep work is increasingly difficult in a world filled with distractions. Developing techniques to enter and maintain this state is essential for maximizing your productivity and achieving your goals.

Techniques for Achieving Flow States

Achieving a flow state requires a combination of preparation, focus, and practice. Here are proven techniques to help you enter and sustain deep work:

1. **Eliminate Distractions:**
   Deep work requires an environment free of interruptions. Create a workspace that minimizes distractions by:
   - Turning off notifications on your devices.
   - Closing unnecessary tabs or applications.
   - Using noise-canceling headphones or white noise.
   - Informing others of your dedicated focus time to prevent interruptions.
2. **Set Clear Objectives:**
   Clarity is crucial for entering a flow state. Before starting, define what you want to achieve during your deep work session. Break larger tasks into smaller, actionable steps to make the process manageable and focused.

Example: Instead of "Write the report," specify, "Write the introduction and outline three key sections of the report."

3.Match Tasks to Skill Level:

Flow occurs when there is a balance between the challenge of the task and your skill level. Tasks that are too easy can lead to boredom, while tasks that are too difficult may cause frustration. Choose tasks that push your limits without overwhelming you.

4.Practice the Pomodoro Technique:

The Pomodoro Technique involves working in focused intervals (typically 25 minutes) followed by short breaks. This method trains your brain to concentrate deeply and prevents burnout.

Action Tip: Use a timer or focus app to structure your deep work sessions, gradually increasing the length of intervals as your focus improves.

1. **Adopt Mindfulness Practices:**

   Mindfulness trains your brain to stay present, making it easier to enter a state of flow. Simple practices like deep breathing, meditation, or journaling before a work session can help calm your mind and prepare you for focused effort.

2. **Use Rituals to Prime Your Mind:**

   Creating a pre-work ritual signals to your brain that it's time to focus. This could be as simple as:
   - Starting your session at the same time each day.
   - Drinking a specific beverage, like coffee or tea.
   - Listening to a particular playlist or white noise.

3. **Leverage Visualization:**

   Visualize yourself successfully completing the task. This mental rehearsal prepares your brain for deep focus and boosts confidence, making it easier to dive into work.

4. **Enter the Zone Gradually:**

   Sometimes, starting a demanding task feels overwhelming. Begin with a low-barrier activity related to the task, such as organizing notes or reviewing background information, to ease into the flow state.

Scheduling Focused Work Time

To consistently engage in deep work, you need to create a structured routine that prioritizes focused work time. Here's how to schedule and protect this valuable time:

1. **Identify Your Peak Productivity Hours:**
   Everyone has natural rhythms of energy and focus. Determine when you feel most alert and creative, and schedule your deep work sessions during these peak hours.

   Action Tip: Track your energy levels for a week to identify patterns and plan your day accordingly.

2. **Use Time Blocking:**
Time blocking involves dedicating specific blocks of time to particular tasks. Block off uninterrupted periods for deep work in your calendar and treat them as non-negotiable appointments with yourself.
   Example:

-
    - 9:00 AM - 11:00 AM: Deep work on presentation.
    - 2:00 PM - 4:00 PM: Deep work on financial analysis.

1. **Start Small and Build Consistency:**
   If you're new to deep work, start with shorter sessions (e.g., 30 minutes) and gradually extend them as your focus improves. Consistency is key to building the habit of sustained focus.
2. **Batch Similar Tasks:**
   Group related tasks into a single session to minimize context

switching. For example, dedicate one session to writing and another to brainstorming.

3. **Plan Breaks Strategically:**
Breaks are essential for maintaining energy and focus over long periods. Use your breaks to recharge by stepping away from your work, stretching, or practicing mindfulness.

Action Tip: Implement the 90/30 Rule: Work for 90 minutes, then take a 30-minute break to refresh.

3.Protect Your Focus Time:
Treat your deep work sessions as sacred. Communicate with colleagues, family, or anyone else who might interrupt you, letting them know that you are unavailable during these periods.

Example: Use status indicators like "Do Not Disturb" on communication apps or physical signs like a closed door to signal your focus time.

4.Review and Reflect:
At the end of each day, review your deep work sessions to evaluate what worked and what didn't. Use this reflection to fine-tune your approach and improve your productivity over time.

Sustaining the Benefits of Deep Work

Engaging in deep work consistently requires effort and discipline, but the rewards are immense. Here's how to sustain the benefits:

- **Track Your Progress:** Keep a journal or use productivity apps to track the tasks you complete during deep work sessions. Seeing your achievements will motivate you to maintain the habit.
- **Celebrate Small Wins:** Acknowledge and reward yourself for completing high-impact tasks during your deep work sessions.
- **Stay Adaptable:** Life can be unpredictable. If your schedule is disrupted, reschedule your deep work time rather than skipping it altogether.

The Transformative Power of Deep Work

Deep work is more than a productivity technique—it's a transformative practice that enables you to produce extraordinary results, develop expertise, and achieve your goals with focus and intention. By mastering the art of achieving flow states and scheduling focused work time, you unlock your brain's full potential and create a life marked by purpose, creativity, and accomplishment.

Chapter 4: Automate and Delegate

Modern life is filled with endless responsibilities, many of which drain our time and energy without contributing significantly to our goals. To reclaim focus and achieve more with less effort, you must master the art of automating and delegating tasks. By outsourcing routine and low-value activities, you free up mental space to concentrate on high-impact work. This chapter explores how to effectively delegate to others and leverage technology to enhance efficiency, empowering you to streamline your workflow and amplify your productivity.

Freeing Up Mental Space by Outsourcing

Delegation is not about shirking responsibility; it is about strategic resource allocation. When you delegate effectively, you empower others to handle tasks that do not require your unique expertise, allowing you to focus on what truly matters.

1. Understanding the Benefits of Delegation

Delegation offers numerous benefits that directly enhance your productivity and mental clarity:

- **Increased Efficiency:** Others may be better suited to handle tasks in areas where they have more expertise or bandwidth.
- **Focus on Core Strengths:** By offloading tasks, you can dedicate your energy to activities that align with your strengths and goals.
- **Reduced Burnout:** Delegating reduces the cognitive load of juggling too many responsibilities.

2. Identifying Delegation Opportunities

To delegate effectively, begin by identifying tasks that can be handled by someone else.

Questions to Ask:

- Does this task require my unique skills or expertise?
- Is this task repetitive or time-consuming?
- Can someone else complete this task with minimal guidance?

Example Tasks for Delegation:

- Administrative work (e.g., scheduling meetings, managing emails).
- Research or data collection.
- Social media management.
- Routine customer support tasks.

3. Choosing the Right Person for the Task

Delegating to the right person ensures tasks are completed efficiently and effectively.

Steps to Choose the Right Delegate:

- **Assess Skills:** Match the task to someone with the necessary skills or experience.
- **Provide Clear Instructions:** Clearly define the task's goals, expected outcomes, and deadlines.
- **Empower Ownership:** Allow the person to take responsibility and make decisions where appropriate.

4. Overcoming Barriers to Delegation

Many people hesitate to delegate due to common fears, such as:

- **Loss of Control:** Trusting someone else with your work can feel risky. However, providing clear guidelines and regular check-ins can mitigate this fear.
- **Belief in Doing It Better:** While it may be true that you can complete the task better or faster, this mindset limits your ability to scale your efforts.

Action Tip: Start small by delegating low-risk tasks and gradually build confidence in the delegation process.

5. Outsourcing Beyond Your Team

In some cases, you may need to outsource tasks to external professionals or services.

- **Freelancers:** Platforms like Upwork or Fiverr provide access to skilled professionals for specific projects.
- **Virtual Assistants:** Hiring a virtual assistant can help with administrative tasks, research, or customer service.
- **Specialized Agencies:** Consider outsourcing marketing, design, or IT needs to agencies with expertise in those areas.

Leveraging Technology for Efficiency

Automation is the ultimate tool for streamlining repetitive tasks and reducing manual effort. By leveraging technology, you can achieve greater efficiency and eliminate unnecessary distractions from your workflow.

1. The Benefits of Automation

Automation frees up time and energy by handling routine tasks, such as:

- Data entry or management.
- Scheduling and reminders.
- Financial tracking and reporting.

Example: Automating your email filtering system ensures important messages land in your inbox while spam and low-priority emails are sorted into separate folders.

2. Tools and Systems for Automation

There are countless tools designed to automate various aspects of your personal and professional life.

Popular Automation Tools:

- **Email Management:** Tools like Gmail filters or Outlook rules automatically organize incoming emails.
- **Scheduling:** Calendly and Doodle simplify scheduling by eliminating back-and-forth communication.
- **Project Management:** Tools like Trello, Asana, or Monday.com allow you to automate task assignments and deadline reminders.
- **Social Media Management:** Platforms like Hootsuite or Buffer enable you to schedule posts and analyze engagement data.

- **Accounting and Invoicing:** QuickBooks or FreshBooks streamline financial tasks.
- **Customer Relationship Management (CRM):** HubSpot and Salesforce automate customer communication and data tracking.

3. Automating Personal Life Tasks

Automation isn't limited to the workplace. You can streamline everyday tasks to reduce mental clutter.

Examples:

- Use smart home devices like Alexa or Google Assistant for reminders, timers, or controlling household appliances.
- Automate bill payments to avoid late fees and reduce the stress of managing finances.
- Set up subscription services for recurring purchases, such as groceries or household supplies.

4. Integrating Technology Seamlessly

The key to successful automation is seamless integration. Your tools should work together to create a unified system.

Action Tip: Use tools like Zapier or IFTTT (If This Then That) to connect different apps and automate workflows. For example, you can automatically save email attachments to a designated Google Drive folder or create tasks in your project management tool from Slack messages.

5. Avoiding Over-Automation

While automation is powerful, it's essential to strike a balance. Over-automating can lead to:

- **Loss of Personal Touch:** In areas like customer communication, overly automated responses can feel impersonal.
- **Complex Systems:** Excessive reliance on automation can create complicated workflows that are hard to manage.

Action Tip: Regularly review your automated systems to ensure they are still effective and aligned with your goals.

Bringing It All Together

Automation and delegation are complementary strategies that enable you to focus on high-value work. By outsourcing tasks to people or technology, you create a streamlined workflow that enhances productivity, reduces stress, and allows you to concentrate on what matters most.

Steps to Implement Automation and Delegation:

1. Audit your current tasks and responsibilities.
2. Identify opportunities for delegation or automation.
3. Select the right tools, systems, or individuals to handle these tasks.
4. Set clear expectations and guidelines for delegated or automated tasks.
5. Regularly evaluate and refine your approach to ensure continued efficiency.

The Ripple Effect of Efficiency

When you master the art of automating and delegating, you not only increase your productivity but also experience significant mental clarity. The time and energy you save can be reinvested into creative pursuits, strategic planning, or personal growth.

Chapter 5: The Results-Driven Life

The results-driven life is a mindset, a lifestyle, and a disciplined approach to achieving meaningful goals. It's not about working endlessly or chasing every opportunity—it's about working smartly, maintaining focus, and creating systems that deliver consistent results over time. In this chapter, we'll explore how to maintain a results-focused mindset for the long term and build robust systems that ensure sustained success.

How to Stay Results-Focused Long-Term

Staying results-focused over time requires more than just willpower; it demands intentional habits, clarity of purpose, and regular reassessment. Here's how to develop and sustain a results-driven approach to life:

1. Start with Your "Why"

Every goal, task, or project should be tied to a clear purpose. Knowing your "why" gives meaning to your efforts, keeps you motivated, and helps you persevere through challenges.

Action Tip: Write a personal mission statement that defines your overarching purpose. Use it as a guidepost for decision-making and goal-setting.

2. Set SMART Goals

Effective goals are Specific, Measurable, Achievable, Relevant, and Time-bound (SMART). Vague aspirations lead to scattered efforts, while well-defined goals provide direction and a clear metric for success.

Example: Instead of "Increase my income," set a goal like, "Earn an additional $1,000 per month within the next six months by starting a side business."

3. Develop a Results-Oriented Mindset

Focus on outcomes, not activities. It's easy to get caught up in being busy, but results come from targeted actions that move you closer to your goals.

Questions to Ask Yourself:

- What is the desired outcome of this task?
- Is this activity the best use of my time to achieve that outcome?

4. Prioritize Consistency Over Perfection

Long-term success doesn't come from occasional bursts of effort but from consistent, incremental progress. Even small steps taken regularly can lead to significant results over time.

Action Tip: Break larger goals into daily or weekly habits. For example, if you want to write a book, commit to writing 500 words a day rather than trying to complete it in a single sprint.

5. Practice Reflection and Reassessment

Regularly evaluate your progress to stay aligned with your goals. Reflection helps you identify what's working, what isn't, and how to adjust your approach for better results.

Action Tip: Schedule weekly or monthly reviews to assess your goals, celebrate achievements, and refine your strategies.

6. Cultivate Discipline and Resilience

Staying results-focused long-term requires discipline to maintain habits and resilience to overcome setbacks. Challenges are inevitable, but your ability to bounce back and stay committed will define your success.

Mantra: "Focus on progress, not perfection."

Building Systems for Sustained Success

Success is not a one-time achievement; it's a continuous process fueled by systems that support your goals. A strong system ensures that you stay productive, focused, and aligned, even when motivation wanes or challenges arise.

1. Create a Routine That Aligns with Your Goals

Routines eliminate decision fatigue and make progress automatic. When you embed goal-oriented actions into your daily routine, success becomes a natural outcome.

Example Routine for a Writer:

- Morning: Write for 90 minutes.
- Afternoon: Research and edit for 60 minutes.
- Evening: Reflect on progress and outline the next day's tasks.

2. Use Time Blocking for Priority Management

Time blocking involves dedicating specific periods of your day to particular tasks. It ensures that your most important activities get the attention they deserve while minimizing distractions.

Action Tip: Divide your day into blocks for deep work, administrative tasks, and personal activities. Honor these blocks as you would appointments.

3. Leverage Productivity Tools

Digital tools can help you stay organized and efficient, allowing you to focus on high-value activities.

Recommended Tools:

- **Task Management:** Trello, Asana, or Notion.
- **Time Tracking:** Toggl or Clockify.
- **Focus Apps:** Forest or Focus@Will.
- **Automation Tools:** Zapier or IFTTT.

4. Build Feedback Loops

Feedback loops provide real-time insights into your progress and help you course-correct.

Example Feedback Loop for Fitness Goals:

- Daily: Track calories and exercise.
- Weekly: Measure weight and fitness improvements.
- Monthly: Adjust diet or workout plan based on results.

5. Delegate and Automate

As discussed in Chapter 4, effective delegation and automation free up mental space and ensure tasks are completed without your constant involvement. These systems allow you to focus on strategic goals while routine activities run on autopilot.

6. Optimize Your Environment for Success

Your environment significantly impacts your ability to stay focused and productive.

Steps to Optimize:

- Remove distractions from your workspace.
- Surround yourself with visual reminders of your goals (e.g., vision boards or motivational quotes).
- Use ergonomics to create a comfortable and efficient setup.

7. Establish Accountability Structures

Accountability keeps you on track by creating external motivation to meet your commitments.

Ways to Build Accountability:

- Join a mastermind group or find an accountability partner.
- Share your goals with a mentor or coach who can provide guidance and encouragement.

- Use public accountability, such as sharing progress updates on social media.

8. Embrace Continuous Learning and Adaptation

The most successful individuals constantly learn and adapt to new challenges and opportunities.

Action Tip: Dedicate time each week to personal development, whether through reading, taking courses, or seeking mentorship.

Sustaining Momentum in the Results-Driven Life

Success is a journey, not a destination. To sustain momentum:

1. **Celebrate Milestones:** Recognizing small wins keeps you motivated and reinforces positive habits.
2. **Stay Flexible:** Life is unpredictable, and rigid systems can become counterproductive. Be willing to adjust your approach as needed.
3. **Avoid Burnout:** Schedule downtime and prioritize self-care to maintain energy and enthusiasm for the long haul.

The Transformation of a Results-Driven Life

By staying results-focused and building systems for sustained success, you create a life of purpose, clarity, and impact. The results-driven life is not about doing more—it's about doing what matters most and doing it well.

As you integrate the principles and strategies outlined in this chapter, you'll find that achieving your goals becomes not only possible but inevitable. The systems you build today will serve as the foundation for a lifetime of progress and fulfillment, empowering you to live intentionally and achieve extraordinary results.

Appendix A: Focus Funnel Templates for Personal and Professional Use

The **Focus Funnel** is a systematic method for filtering tasks and determining where to allocate your time and energy. By applying its principles, you can effectively eliminate, automate, delegate, or prioritize tasks that require your attention. This appendix provides ready-to-use templates for both personal and professional scenarios, helping you streamline decision-making and maintain focus.

How to Use the Focus Funnel

1. **Eliminate:** Ask, "Does this task truly need to be done?" If the answer is no, eliminate it.
2. **Automate:** If the task is necessary but repetitive, explore tools or processes that can handle it automatically.
3. **Delegate:** If the task requires human intervention but doesn't need your expertise, delegate it to someone else.
4. **Prioritize:** If the task survives all filters, it's a high-priority item deserving your direct attention.

Template 1: Personal Focus Funnel

This template helps you apply the Focus Funnel method to personal tasks, such as household chores, health goals, or personal development projects.

Step 1: List Your Tasks

Write down all tasks or responsibilities currently on your plate.

Example:

- Grocery shopping
- Scheduling doctor's appointment
- Responding to family emails

- Planning a weekend trip
- Organizing closets

Step 2: Apply the Focus Funnel

Task	Eliminate?	Automate?	Delegate?	Prioritize?	Notes
Grocery shopping	No	Yes (use online delivery apps)	No	No	Automate with weekly delivery service.
Scheduling doctor's appointment	No	Yes (use scheduling apps)	No	No	Automate using the clinic's app.
Responding to family emails	No	No	Yes (delegate updates to a family member)	No	Delegate to spouse or sibling.
Planning a weekend trip	No	No	No	Yes	Requires personal attention.
Organizing closets	Yes	No	No	No	Eliminate or reschedule for later.

Template 2: Professional Focus Funnel

Use this template for tasks in your professional life, such as managing projects, attending meetings, or handling emails.

Step 1: List Your Tasks

Write down all tasks currently assigned to you at work.

Example:

- Preparing a presentation for a client
- Attending weekly status meetings
- Responding to team emails
- Managing project timelines
- Generating monthly reports

Step 2: Apply the Focus Funnel

Task	Eliminate?	Automate?	Delegate?	Prioritize?	Notes
Preparing a presentation	No	No	No	Yes	High-priority task, requires creativity.
Attending weekly meetings	No	No	Yes (ask for meeting notes)	No	Delegate to a team member.
Responding to team emails	No	Yes (use email templates)	No	No	Automate with pre-written responses.

Task	Eliminate?	Automate?	Delegate?	Prioritize?	Notes
Managing project timelines	No	Yes (use project management tools)	No	No	Automate using Trello or Asana.
Generating monthly reports	No	Yes (use reporting software)	Yes	No	Automate with Excel macros or software.

Template 3: Hybrid Personal and Professional Focus Funnel

This template is ideal for individuals who juggle personal and professional responsibilities, such as entrepreneurs, freelancers, or remote workers.

Step 1: List Your Tasks

Combine personal and professional tasks into one list.

Example:

- Writing a blog post
- Paying utility bills
- Attending a client call
- Preparing dinner
- Reviewing monthly finances

Step 2: Apply the Focus Funnel

Task	Eliminate?	Automate?	Delegate?	Prioritize?	Notes
Writing a blog post	No	No	No	Yes	Creative work requires focus.
Paying utility bills	No	Yes (set up auto-pay)	No	No	Automate through bank or service apps.

Task	Eliminate?	Automate?	Delegate?	Prioritize?	Notes
Attending a client call	No	No	No	Yes	Client-facing task needs personal touch.
Preparing dinner	No	No	Yes (order meal kits)	No	Delegate to a family member or service.
Reviewing monthly finances	No	Yes (use financial software)	No	Yes	Automate data input with budgeting tools.

Tools for Automation

The following tools can be used to streamline repetitive tasks and implement the automation step of the Focus Funnel effectively:

Personal Automation Tools

- **Grocery Shopping:** Instacart, Amazon Fresh
- **Bill Payments:** Bank auto-pay, PayPal, Venmo
- **Appointments:** Calendly, Google Calendar

Professional Automation Tools

- **Email Management:** Gmail filters, Outlook rules
- **Project Management:** Asana, Trello, Monday.com

- **Reporting and Analytics:** Microsoft Excel macros, Google Data Studio
- **Client Communication:** HubSpot, Salesforce

Checklist for Implementing the Focus Funnel

Use this checklist to ensure every task goes through the Focus Funnel process:

1. **Eliminate:**
   - Is this task necessary for achieving my goals?
   - Can I avoid this task without negative consequences?
2. **Automate:**
   - Can technology handle this task efficiently?
   - Is there a tool or app available for this process?
3. **Delegate:**
   - Who has the skills to take over this task?
   - Can I provide clear instructions and set expectations?
4. **Prioritize:**
   - Is this task aligned with my long-term goals?
   - Does this task require my unique expertise or creativity?

Final Thoughts

The Focus Funnel is not just a decision-making framework—it's a lifestyle. By consistently applying this method, you can reduce overwhelm, enhance productivity, and focus your energy on what truly matters. Use the templates and tools provided in this appendix to streamline your personal and professional tasks, ensuring that every action you take aligns with your goals and delivers meaningful results.

<u>Message from the Author:</u>

I hope you enjoyed this book, I love astrology and knew there was not a book such as this out on the shelf. I love metaphysical items as well. Please check out my other books:

-Life of Government Benefits

-My life of Hell

-My life with Hydrocephalus

-Red Sky

-World Domination:Woman's rule

-World Domination:Woman's Rule 2: The War

-Life and Banishment of Apophis: book 1

-The Kidney Friendly Diet

-The Ultimate Hemp Cookbook

-Creating a Dispensary(legally)

-Cleanliness throughout life: the importance of showering from childhood to adulthood.

-Strong Roots: The Risks of Overcoddling children

-Hemp Horoscopes: Cosmic Insights and Earthly Healing

- Celestial Hemp Navigating the Zodiac: Through the Green Cosmos

-Astrological Hemp: Aligning The Stars with Earth's Ancient Herb

-The Astrological Guide to Hemp: Stars, Signs, and Sacred Leaves

-Green Growth: Innovative Marketing Strategies for your Hemp Products and Dispensary

-Cosmic Cannabis

-Astrological Munchies

-Henry The Hemp

-Zodiacal Roots: The Astrological Soul Of Hemp

- Green Constellations: Intersection of Hemp and Zodiac

-Hemp in The Houses: An astrological Adventure Through The Cannabis Galaxy

-Galactic Ganja Guide

Heavenly Hemp

Zodiac Leaves

Doctor Who Astrology

Cannastrology

Stellar Satvias and Cosmic Indicas

Celestial Cannabis: A Zodiac Journey

AstroHerbology: The Sky and The Soil: Volume 1

AstroHerbology:Celestial Cannabis:Volume 2

Cosmic Cannabis Cultivation

The Starry Guide to Herbal Harmony: Volume 1

The Starry Guide to Herbal Harmony: Cannabis Universe: Volume 2

Yugioh Astrology: Astrological Guide to Deck, Duels and more

Nightmare Mansion: Echoes of The Abyss

Nightmare Mansion 2: Legacy of Shadows

Nightmare Mansion 3: Shadows of the Forgotten

Nightmare Mansion 4: Echoes of the Damned

The Life and Banishment of Apophis: Book 2

Nightmare Mansion: Halls of Despair

Healing with Herb: Cannabis and Hydrocephalus

Planetary Pot: Aligning with Astrological Herbs: Volume 1

Fast Track to Freedom: 30 Days to Financial Independence Using AI, Assets, and Agile Hustles

Cosmic Hemp Pathways

How to Become Financially Free in 30 Days: 10,000 Paths to Prosperity

Zodiacal Herbage: Astrological Insights: Volume 1

Nightmare Mansion: Whispers in the Walls

The Daleks Invade Atlantis

Henry the hemp and Hydrocephalus

10X The Kidney Friendly Diet

Cannabis Universe: Adult coloring book

Hemp Astrology: The Healing Power of the Stars

Zodiacal Herbage: Astrological Insights: Cannabis Universe: Volume 2

<u>Planetary Pot: Aligning with Astrological Herbs: Cannabis Universes: Volume 2</u>

Doctor Who Meets the Replicators and SG-1: The Ultimate Battle for Survival

Nightmare Mansion: Curse of the Blood Moon

<u>The Celestial Stoner: A Guide to the Zodiac</u>

Cosmic Pleasures: Sex Toy Astrology for Every Sign

Hydrocephalus Astrology: Navigating the Stars and Healing Waters

Lapis and the Mischievous Chocolate Bar

Celestial Positions: Sexual Astrology for Every Sign

Apophis's Shadow Work Journal: : A Journey of Self-Discovery and Healing

Kinky Cosmos: Sexual Kink Astrology for Every Sign

Digital Cosmos: The Astrological Digimon Compendium

Stellar Seeds: The Cosmic Guide to Growing with Astrology

Apophis's Daily Gratitude Journal

Cat Astrology: Feline Mysteries of the Cosmos

The Cosmic Kama Sutra: An Astrological Guide to Sexual Positions

Unleash Your Potential: A Guided Journal Powered by AI Insights

Whispers of the Enchanted Grove

Cosmic Pleasures: An Astrological Guide to Sexual Kinks

369, 12 Manifestation Journal

Whisper of the nocturne journal(blank journal for writing or drawing)

The Boogey Book

Locked In Reflection: A Chastity Journey Through Locktober

Generating Wealth Quickly:

How to Generate $100,000 in 24 Hours

Star Magic: Harness the Power of the Universe

The Flatulence Chronicles: A Fart Journal for Self-Discovery

The Doctor and The Death Moth

Seize the Day: A Personal Seizure Tracking Journal

The Ultimate Boogeyman Safari: A Journey into the Boogie World and Beyond

Whispers of Samhain: 1,000 Spells of Love, Luck, and Lunar Magic: Samhain Spell Book

Apophis's guides:

Witch's Spellbook Crafting Guide for Halloween

<u>Frost & Flame: The Enchanted Yule Grimoire of 1000 Winter Spells</u>

<u>The Ultimate Boogey Goo Guide & Spooky Activities for Halloween Fun</u>

Harmony of the Scales: A Libra's Spellcraft for Balance and Beauty

The Enchanted Advent: 36 Days of Christmas Wonders

Nightmare Mansion: The Labyrinth of Screams

Harvest of Enchantment: 1,000 Spells of Gratitude, Love, and Fortune for Thanksgiving

The Boogey Chronicles: A Journal of Nightly Encounters and Shadowy Secrets

The 12 Days of Financial Freedom: A Step-by-Step Christmas Countdown to Transform Your Finances

Sigil of the Eternal Spiral Blank Journal

A Christmas Feast: Timeless Recipes for Every Meal

Holiday Stress-Free Solutions: A Survival Guide to Thriving During the Festive Season

Yu-Gi-Oh! Holiday Gifting Mastery: The Ultimate Guide for Fans and Newcomers Alike

Holiday Harmony: A Hydrocephalus Survival Guide for the Festive Season

Celestial Craft: The Witch's Almanac for 2025 – A Cosmic Guide to Manifestations, Moons, and Mystical Events

Doctor Who: The Toymaker's Winter Wonderland

Tulsa King Unveiled: A Thrilling Guide to Stallone's Mafia Masterpiece

Pendulum Craft: A Complete Guide to Crafting and Using Personalized Divination Tools

Nightmare Mansion: Santa's Eternal Eve

Starlight Noel: A Cosmic Journey through Christmas Mysteries

The Dark Architect: Unlocking the Blueprint of Existence

Surviving the Embrace: The Ultimate Guide to Encounters with The Hugging Molly

The Enchanted Codex: Secrets of the Craft for Witches, Wiccans, and Pagans

Harvest of Gratitude: A Complete Thanksgiving Guide

Yuletide Essentials: A Complete Guide to an Authentic and Magical Christmas

Celestial Smokes: A Cosmic Guide to Cigars and Astrology

Living in Balance: A Comprehensive Survival Guide to Thriving with Diabetes Insipidus

Cosmic Symbiosis: The Venom Zodiac Chronicles

The Cursed Paw of Ambition

Cosmic Symbiosis: The Astrological Venom Journal

Celestial Wonders Unfold: A Stargazer's Guide to the Cosmos (2024-2029)

The Ultimate Black Friday Prepper's Guide: Mastering Shopping Strategies and Savings

Cosmic Sales: The Astrological Guide to Black Friday Shopping

Legends of the Corn Mother and Other Harvest Myths

Whispers of the Harvest: The Corn Mother's Journal

The Evergreen Spellbook

The Doctor Meets the Boogeyman

The White Witch of Rose Hall's SpellBook

The Gingerbread Golem's Shadow: A Study in Sweet Darkness

The Gingerbread Golem Codex: An Academic Exploration of Sweet Myths

The Gingerbread Golem Grimoire: Sweet Magicks and Spells for the Festive Witch

The Curse of the Gingerbread Golem

10-minute Christmas Crafts for kids

<u>Christmas Crisis Solutions: The Ultimate Last-Minute Survival Guide</u>

Gingerbread Golem Recipes: Holiday Treats with a Magical Twist

The Infinite Key: Unlocking Mystical Secrets of the Ages

Enchanted Yule: A Wiccan and Pagan Guide to a Magical and Memorable Season

Dinosaurs of Power: Unlocking Ancient Magick

Astro-Dinos: The Cosmic Guide to Prehistoric Wisdom

Gallifrey's Yule Logs: A Festive Doctor Who Cookbook

The Dino Grimoire: Secrets of Prehistoric Magick

The Gift They Never Knew They Needed

The Gingerbread Golem's Culinary Alchemy: Enchanting Recipes for a Sweetly Dark Feast

A Time Lord Christmas: Holiday Adventures with the Doctor

Krampusproofing Your Home: Defensive Strategies for Yule

Silent Frights: A Collection of Christmas Creepypastas to Chill Your Bones

Santa Raptor's Jolly Carnage: A Dino-Claus Christmas Tale

Prehistoric Palettes: A Dino Wicca Coloring Journey

The Christmas Wishkeeper Chronicles

The Starlight Sleigh: A Holiday Journey

Elf Secrets: The True Magic of the North Pole

Candy Cane Conjurations

Cooking with Kids: Recipes Under 20 Minutes

Doctor Who: The TARDIS Confiscation

The Anxiety First Aid Kit: Quick Tools to Calm Your Mind

Frosty Whispers: A Winter's Tale

The Infinite Key: Unlocking the Secrets to Prosperity, Resilience, and Purpose

The Grasping Void: Why You'll Regret This Purchase

Astrology for Busy Bees: Star Signs Simplified

The Instant Focus Formula: Cut Through the Noise

The Secret Language of Colors: Unlocking the Emotional Codes

Sacred Fossil Chronicles: Blank Journal

The Christmas Cottage Miracle

Feeding Frenzy: Graboid-Inspired Recipes

Manifest in Minutes: The Quick Law of Attraction Guide

The Symbiote Chronicles: Doctor Who's Venomous Journey

Think Tiny, Grow Big: The Minimalist Mindset

The Energy Key: Unlocking Limitless Motivation

New Year, New Magic: Manifesting Your Best Year Yet

Unstoppable You: Mastering Confidence in Minutes

Infinite Energy: The Secret to Never Feeling Drained

Lightning Focus: Mastering the Art of Productivity in a Distracted World

Saturnalia Manifestation Magick: A Guide to Unlocking Abundance During the Solstice

Graboids and Garland: The Ultimate Tremors-Themed Christmas Guide

12 Nights of Holiday Magic

The Power of Pause: 60-Second Mindfulness Practices

The Quick Reset: How to Reclaim Your Life After Burnout

The Shadow Eater: A Tale of Despair and Survival

If you want solar for your home go here: https://www.harborso-lar.live/apophisenterprises/

Get Some Tarot cards: https://www.makeplayingcards.com/sell/ apophis-occult-shop

<u>**Get some shirts:** https://www.bonfire.com/store/apophis-shirt-emporium/</u>

<u>**Instagrams:**</u>
@apophis_enterprises,
@apophisbookemporium,
@apophisscardshop
Twitter: @apophisenterpr1
Tiktok:@apophisenterprise
Youtube: @sg1fan23477, @FiresideRetreatKingdom
Hive: @sg1fan23477
CheeLee: @SG1fan23477

Podcast: Apophis Chat Zone: https://open.spotify.com/show/5zXbrCLEV2xzCp8ybrfHsk?si=fb4d4fdbdce44dec

Newsletter: https://apophiss-newsletter-27c897.beehiiv.com/

If you want to support me or see posts of other projects that I have come over to: **buymeacoffee.com/mpetchinskg**
I post there daily several times a day

Get your Dinowicca or Christmas themed digital products, especially Santa Raptor songs and other musics. Here:
https://sg1fan23477.gumroad.com

Apophis Yuletide Digital has not only digital Christmas items, but it will have all things with Dinowicca as well as other Digital products.

www.ingramcontent.com/pod-product-compliance
Lightning Source LLC
Chambersburg PA
CBHW060914130726

48001CB00006B/2237